ANIMALS BEHAVING BADLY

by Jessica Fries-Gaither

Millbrook Press / Minneapolis

You've heard grown-ups say it again and again.

Mind your manners.

Be polite.

Be on your best behavior.

And that's important—for us humans.

But for some animals, bad manners are a way of life.

Grown-ups say,

Always tell the truth.

But in the animal world, lies aren't always bad.

Scarlet kingsnakes pretend to be someone else.

SCARLET KINGSNAKES don't have fangs. Instead, they constrict, or squeeze, to kill their prey. That makes scarlet kingsnakes easier targets for predators than other snakes. To protect themselves, they have evolved to look like the venomous eastern coral snake. Their red, black, and yellow banding tells potential predators that they are dangerous (though it's not true). The predators stay away. The snake's fib is an adaptation called mimicry.

Female fireflies deceive other males.

Female *Photuris* firefly (right) feeding on a male firefly (left).

FEMALE *PHOTURIS* FIREFLIES copy the unique flashing patterns of other firefly groups. When a male of a different firefly species responds and gets close, the female eats him by sucking his blood and then devouring his body.

When an **EASTERN HOGNOSE SNAKE** is threatened, it writhes around for a few seconds then lies belly-up, mouth hanging open, and tongue sticking out to the side. By pretending to be dead—a behavior scientists call thanatosis—the snake tries to convince the potential predator to leave it alone.

Eastern hognose snakes fake their own deaths.

Grown-ups say,

Be fair and play by the rules.

But for some crafty creatures, cheating is a way of life.

Brown-headed cowbirds con other species into raising their chicks.

When a **FEMALE COWBIRD** is ready to lay an egg, she searches for another bird's nest and damages or removes one or more eggs. Then she replaces the missing eggs with her own. Brown-headed cowbird chicks hatch faster and are often larger than other baby birds, so they get more food and resources from their caretakers.

brown-headed cowbird

Black garden ants hypnotize aphids into sticking around.

BLACK GARDEN ANTS feed on the sugary honeydew that aphids produce. The ants use several sneaky methods to keep the aphids nearby their nests. They bite off the aphids' wings and put a chemical on their feet that acts as a tranquilizer to keep the aphids calm.

CROWS give warning calls to alert other crows of danger. But some cunning crows will issue fake calls to scare their competition away from food.

Crows give false alarms.

Grown-ups say,

Don't take things that aren't yours.

But some animals have sticky beaks and paws.

Chinstrap penguins steal from their neighbors.

CHINSTRAP PENGUINS build nests from rocks for the breeding season. But the work doesn't stop once the nests are built. When the penguins aren't incubating their eggs, they steal rocks from their neighbors' nests and add them to their own. Scientists think larger nests are less likely to flood and are safer for hatching and fledging chicks.

Lions and spotted hyenas swipe each other's dinners.

LIONS and **SPOTTED HYENAS** live in the same habitats, hunt the same prey, and scavenge the same animal remains. Food can be hard to come by on the African savannah, so they steal each other's kills and scraps quite often—a behavior called kleptoparasitism.

Male **BOWERBIRDS** attract mates by building elaborate structures called bowers out of sticks. They decorate them with everything from stones and feathers to objects people have dropped. But the males go one step further to win a female's attention. They steal objects from their competitors' bowers and even destroy the bowers altogether.

Bowerbirds do more than borrow.

Grown-ups say,

Keep yourself neat and clean.

But some animals have terrible personal hygiene.

Turkey vultures poop themselves on purpose.

TURKEY VULTURES have an unusual strategy to stay cool in hot weather. They poop on their own feet. Bird droppings are a mixture of feces and urine. As the liquid evaporates from the droppings, it helps to cool the bird—just like sweating keeps you cool on a hot day. The liquid is also a foot sanitizer, keeping the bird safe from harmful bacteria that might be in the animal carcasses it feeds on.

turkey vulture

Baby **EUROPEAN ROLLERS** vomit a stinky orange liquid on themselves when scared by predators. In addition to convincing the predators to leave them alone, the smell warns the parents that the nest is in danger.

European rollers cover themselves with puke.

Hippos throw their waste around.

Male **HIPPOS** defend their territory by spinning their tails around like propellers, flinging poop and pee in all directions. Sometimes simply hearing the calls of unfamiliar hippos is enough to start a dung shower.

Grown-ups say,

Be a gracious house guest.

But some animals are the worst!

The tongue-eating louse moves in and never leaves.

A **TONGUE-EATING LOUSE** attaches itself to the base of a fish's tongue and cuts the blood vessels inside. Next it sucks the blood out until the tongue drops off and then the louse attaches itself to the remaining stump. Surprisingly, this doesn't kill the fish. The louse lives the rest of its life in the fish's mouth, where it stays protected and feeds off the fish's blood and mucus.

The braconid wasp eats its host out of house and home.

BRACONID WASPS are parasites that infect tomato and tobacco hornworm caterpillars. The female wasp uses her extra-long ovipositor to inject eggs into the host caterpillar's body. After the wasp larvae hatch, the hungry babies eat the caterpillar from the inside out, finally bursting out to build cocoons on the outside of the caterpillar's body.

Warble flies worm their way into caribou.

In midsummer, female **WARBLE FLIES** land on caribou and lay a sticky package of eggs. After hatching, the maggots tunnel through the caribou's skin and make their way toward the spine. They spend the winter feeding on the caribou's flesh and breathing through a hole they carve in its back. In the spring, the maggots leave the caribou's body and develop into adults. The caribou's wounds are easily infected.

Caribou are warble flies' unwilling hosts.

Grown-ups say,

Never, ever be a bully.

But some animals can be quite mean.

Sea otters hold others' babies hostage.

MALE SEA OTTERS sometimes snatch a female's pup and hold it underwater, as if trying to drown it, while the female is hunting for food. When the female hands over the food, the male lets go of the pup.

Dolphins beat up their smaller cousins.

Although **DOLPHINS** look happy and playful, they can be quite aggressive with porpoises. Dolphins have been spotted harassing, attacking, and even killing their smaller cousins. Scientists have even coined a name for the behavior: porpicide. They aren't sure why dolphins do this.

KELP GULLS and **DOLPHIN GULLS** eat the poop of South American fur seal pups that is infected with hookworms. Sometimes the gulls get too eager for their meal and stab their beaks into the seal pups' bottoms. Ouch!

Seagulls don't keep their beaks to themselves.

Whether they lie, cheat, or steal, you might think that these animals have no manners.

But those behaviors we call "rude" actually help them survive.

A BIT ABOUT ANIMAL BEHAVIOR

Whether they live in groups or alone, animals interact with others of their species and with other species at different times. Those interactions might be random or on purpose, short or long, positive or negative. Scientists who study animal behavior, ethologists, try to understand how animals interact with each other and why they behave the way they do.

Animals' behaviors usually meet one of their needs. Hunting, for example, helps an animal meet its need for food. So does stealing food from another animal. Even though we think this is rude behavior, to the animal, it is simply a way to survive. Other behaviors don't help an animal meet its own needs, but instead help its offspring, or babies, survive.

Animals that live in groups often exhibit different behaviors than animals that live alone. They are more likely to cooperate, share resources, and care for each other. These types of behaviors keep the group together. In some groups, individual animals have different social positions and jobs. Each individual contributes to the well-being of the group.

There are always exceptions, though. Sometimes we cannot find reasons for animals' behavior. For example, scientists aren't really sure why dolphins are so aggressive to porpoises. And sometimes, animal behaviors come and go. One example happened years ago in the Pacific Ocean. One orca whale swam around with a dead salmon on its head, like a hat. Others in her pod began doing it, too, for the rest of the summer. The next year? No salmon hats. Scientists still don't know why the trend started—or ended. Then in 2024, the orcas once again appeared wearing the hats.

Understanding animal behavior is tricky. It's tempting to give animals our human thoughts and emotions, and we do this all the time without thinking about it. Listen to people talk about their pets or the animals at the zoo, and you'll hear it over and over again. But we can't assume that animals think and react exactly like we do. While new technology is helping scientists learn more, there's still so much that we don't know. Maybe you'll help us understand animal behavior better in the future!

GLOSSARY

breeding (BREE-ding): mating and having babies

constrict (kuhn-STRIKT): to squeeze tightly

evolve (ee-VAHLV): to change slowly over time

feces (FEE-seez): poop

fledging (FLEH-jing): leaving the nest after reaching a certain stage of maturity

foster (FAH-stir): to raise young that are not one's own through birth

incubate (IN-kyuh-bayt): to keep something warm and safe so it can develop and grow

kleptoparasitism (KLEP-toh-PAIR-uh-SIH-TI-zuhm): when one animal deliberately steals food from another animal

maggot (MAY-guht): the soft, legless young that eventually turns into a fly

mimicry (MIH-mih-kree): when one living thing closely resembles another

ovipositor (OH-vuh-PAH-zuh-tuhr): a tubelike organ used by some insects to lay eggs

parasite (PAIR-uh-sayt): an animal that lives on or in another animal and harms it in some way

predator (PREH-duh-tuhr): an animal that hunts and eats another animal

thanatosis (THA-nuh-TOH-sis): when an animal fakes its own death to avoid harm

tranquilizer (TRANG-kwa-LY-zuhr): a chemical that makes a living thing calm and quiet

urine (YUHR-ihn): pee

venomous (VEH-nuh-muhs): an animal that produces poison

FURTHER READING

Books

Guibert, Grace. *What a Jerk!* Chicago: World Book, 2018.

Keating, Jess. *Gross as a Snot Otter: Discovering the World's Most Disgusting Animals.* New York: Knopf, 2019.

Masoff, Joy. *Oh, Ick!: 114 Science Experiments Guaranteed to Gross You Out.* New York: Workman Publishing, 2016.

Montgomery, Heather L. *How Rude!: 10 Real Bugs Who Won't Mind Their Manners.* Illustrated by Howard McWilliam. New York: Scholastic, 2015.

Tekavec, Heather. *Wanted!: Criminals of the Animal Kingdom.* Illustrated by Susan Batori. Toronto: Kids Can Press, 2020.

Websites

https://kids.nationalgeographic.com/animals

https://pbskids.org/wildkratts/creaturepedia

https://rangerrick.org

You can find the complete bibliography of sources consulted at https://www.jessicafriesgaither.com/so-rude.

For Zaden and Zac, with love
–JFG

Millbrook Press™
An imprint of Lerner Publishing Group, Inc.
241 First Avenue North
Minneapolis, MN 55401 USA

For reading levels and more information, look up this title at www.lernerbooks.com.

Designed by Emily Harris.
Main body text set in Tw Cen MT Std. Typeface provided by Monotype Typography.

Image credits: monkeybusinessimages/Getty Images, pp. 2–3; Ethan Ramirez/Getty Images, pp. 4–5; Radiant Reptilia/Shutterstock, p. 5 (bottom); Nature Picture Library/Alamy, pp. 6, 23; © Maquitico Y, Vergara A, Villanueva I, Camacho J, Cordero C (CC BY 4.0), p. 6 (top); Ed Reschke/Getty Images, p. 7; Science History Images/Alamy, pp. 8–9; Stan Tekiela/Getty Images, p. 9 (bottom); simon skidmore/Alamy, p. 10; Merrimon/Getty Images, p. 11; robertharding/Alamy, pp. 12–13; Londolozi Images/Mint Images/Getty Images, p. 14; JohnCarnemolla/Getty Images, p. 15; All Canada Photos/Alamy, pp. 16–17; Phil Seu Photography/Getty Images, p. 17 (bottom); TAMER YILMAZ/Getty Images, p. 18; Russell Watkins/Alamy, p. 19; Media Drum World/Alamy, p. 21; Scott Camazine/Alamy, p. 22; Dennis Welker/Getty Images, p. 23 (bottom); Hal Beral/Getty Images, pp. 24–25; slowmotiongli/Getty Images, p. 26; Raimund Linke/Getty Images, p. 27; Henrik Karlsson/Getty Images, pp. 28–29; by wildestanimal/Getty Images, p. 30.
Cover: Chris Gomersall/Alamy.

Library of Congress Cataloging-in-Publication Data

Names: Fries-Gaither, Jessica, 1977– author
Title: So rude! : animals behaving badly / Jessica Fries-Gaither.
Other titles: Animals behaving badly
Description: Minneapolis : Millbrook Press, [2026] | Includes bibliographical references. | Audience: Ages 4–9 | Audience: Grades 2–3 | Summary: "Humans have many rules for how to behave, but for animals, breaking those rules can be a matter of survival. Meet rule-breaking animals including kingsnakes, hippos, bowerbirds, and many more!"— Provided by publisher.
Identifiers: LCCN 2024055807 (print) | LCCN 2024055808 (ebook) | ISBN 9798765671047 lib. bdg. | ISBN 9798765682616 epub
Subjects: LCSH: Animal behavior—Juvenile literature | Ritualization—Juvenile literature
Classification: LCC QL751.5 .F738 2026 (print) | LCC QL751.5 (ebook) | DDC 591.5—dc23/eng/20250324

LC record available at https://lccn.loc.gov/2024055807
LC ebook record available at https://lccn.loc.gov/2024055808

Manufactured in the United States of America
1-1012029-54143-4/3/2025